BOOKS AND READING
A Book of Quotations

BOOKS AND READING
A Book of Quotations

DOVER THRIFT EDITIONS

Edited by
Bill Bradfield

DOVER PUBLICATIONS, INC.
MINEOLA, NEW YORK

DOVER THRIFT EDITIONS

GENERAL EDITOR: PAUL NEGRI
EDITOR OF THIS VOLUME: TOM CRAWFORD

Bibliographical Note

Books and Reading: A Book of Quotations is a new work, first published
by Dover Publications, Inc., in 2002.

Library of Congress Cataloging-in-Publication Data

Books and reading : a book of quotations / [compiled by] Bill Bradfield.
　　p. cm.
　ISBN-13: 978-0-486-42463-7
　ISBN-10: 0-486-42463-4 (pbk.)

　　1. Books and reading—Quotations, maxims, etc. I. Bradfield, Bill,
1927–

PN6084.B65 B65 2002
028—dc21

2002025660

Manufactured in the United States by RR Donnelley
42463405　　2016
www.doverpublications.com

Note

IN AN AGE of proliferating electronic books, videos, DVDs, and other non-print media, the traditional book still retains its peculiar power and appeal. Its portability, relatively low cost, and comforting tactile presence set the book apart. After all, it's hard to curl up with a computer monitor. Moreover, a well-made book, carefully designed, with fine binding, well-chosen typography and illustrations, can be a work of art. As George Bernard Shaw put it, "There is nothing on earth more exquisite than a bonny book, with well-placed columns of rich black writing in beautiful borders, and illuminated pictures cunningly inset."

Inextricably intertwined with the book are the pleasures and benefits of reading. Without leaving your chair, you can travel the world, engage in a silent dialogue with the greatest minds in history, plumb the sublime depths of Shakespeare's poetry, or the depths of the sea with Jules Verne, acquire a skill, enjoy the world's great art, discover a wealth of facts and information, and perhaps most important, discover yourself. Anna Quindlen puts it this way: "In books I have traveled, not only to other worlds, but into my own. I learned who I was and who I wanted to be, what I might aspire to, and what I might dare to dream about my world and myself."

The above quotations, along with 448 others, will be found in this carefully selected collection of trenchant observations spanning many centuries and a broad range of readers—from Cicero

to Oprah Winfrey. Ranging from hilarious to heartfelt, from
zany to profound, these quotations are not only wonderful brows-
ing material for book lovers, they offer a mine of usable material
in which teachers, librarians, public speakers—anyone in need
of a bibliophilic bon mot—can find just the right remark.
The quotations are arranged alphabetically by author for ease of
reference.

A book never bores you because you can always lay it down before it becomes a bore.

LYMAN ABBOTT

When I was playing professional basketball, all I had time and energy to do when I was on the road was read. We might have a two-hour practice during the day and then the rest of the time we'd be sitting around the hotel, so I filled those hours with reading. I realized I had to rest a lot and eat well in order to play basketball well, so I wasn't a huge party animal on the road . . . Reading helped me pass the time in a productive way that kept my mind expanding, and kept adding something to my life.

KAREEM ABDUL-JABBAR

I find that a great part of the information I have was acquired by looking up something and finding something else along the way.

FRANKLIN P. ADAMS

Of all the diversions of life, there is none so proper to fill up its empty spaces as the reading of useful and entertaining authors.

JOSEPH ADDISON

In the case of good books, the point is not to see how many of them you can get through, but rather how many can get through to you.

The great books are not merely a record of civilization, but the most potent civilizing force in the world today.

MORTIMER ADLER

Rolando de Aguiar, executive vice president and chief financial officer of Ames Department Stores, a retail discount chain in the northeastern U.S., told a *Wall Street Journal* columnist that he's putting much more time into reading and networking to keep up with new trends, adding: "You have to be conscious of doing it on a daily basis. A few years ago you could take a Peter Drucker book and read it and that could drive you for the next five years. Now you take a dot.com book and read it and you better read another one six months from now because it will be out of date."

ROLANDO DE AGUIAR

Read the great stuff but read the stuff that isn't so great, too. Great stuff is very discouraging. If you read only Beckett and Chekhov, you'll go away and only deliver telegrams for Western Union.

EDWARD ALBEE

I get most of my story ideas poking about in library stacks, on the lookout for books that interest me . . . Reading is serendipitous. The past is there to be mined, and the quirky stories are the ones to pursue.

CAROLINE ALEXANDER, offering advice
to aspiring nonfiction authors

He writes so well he makes me feel like putting my quill back in my goose.

FRED ALLEN

I read a book twice as fast as anybody else. First I read the beginning, and then I read the ending, and then I start in the middle and read toward whichever end I like best.

GRACIE ALLEN

I took a course in speed reading, learning to read straight down the middle of the page, and was able to read *War and Peace* in twenty minutes. It's about Russia.

I'm a voracious reader. You have to read to survive. People who read for pleasure are wasting their time. Reading isn't fun, it's indispensable.

WOODY ALLEN

Without sufficient money for a meal I have spent the few pence I possessed to obtain from a library one of Scott's novels, and, reading it, forgot hunger and cold, and felt myself rich and happy.

HANS CHRISTIAN ANDERSEN

One of the more enlightening truths one learns from books is the exacting presence of the mystery of life.

ANONYMOUS

Beware of the man of one book.

SAINT THOMAS AQUINAS

LIBRARY

Here is where people,
One frequently finds,
Lower their voices
And raise their minds.

RICHARD ARMOUR

Books are still man's greatest invention, despite the nonsense so often published between their covers.

MARTIN ARNOLD

Some books are undeservedly forgotten; none are undeservedly remembered.

W. H. AUDEN

I prefer bread and water with books, to the best of eating without them.

STEPHEN F. AUSTIN, inscribed in his journal in 1834, as he languished in a Mexico City prison

Reading maketh a full man . . . If he read little, he had need have much cunning, to seem to know that he doth not.

Some books are to be tasted, others to be swallowed, and some few to be chewed and digested . . . Histories make men wise, poets witty, the mathematics subtile, natural philosophy deep, moral grave, logic and rhetoric able to contend.

FRANCIS BACON

Do not try reading this book from cover to cover. Except for computer manuals and high school operetta, there is nothing more deadening than an uninterrupted diet of humor.

RUSSELL BAKER, introducing
Russell Baker's Book of American Humor

He has only half learned the art of reading who has not added to it the more refined art of skipping and skimming.

ARTHUR JAMES BALFOUR

The ancient Egyptian had a profound belief in the magical virtue of the written word, and one of his favorite ways of possessing himself of the knowledge was to wash off in beer the writing of any roll whose contents he wished to make infallibly his own, subsequently drinking the beer. He thus literally absorbed the knowledge which he desired to possess.

JAMES BALKIE

Books are where things are explained to you. Life is where things are not.

JULIAN BARNES

Software is usually accompanied by documentation in the form of big scary manuals that nobody ever reads. In fact, for the past five years, most of the "manuals" shipped with software products have actually been copies of Stephen King's *The Stand* with new covers pasted on.

DAVE BARRY

Without books, God is silent, justice dormant, natural science at a stand, philosophy lame, letters dumb, and all things involved in darkness.

THOMAS V. BARTHOLIN

The true reader allows himself a balanced diet and moves easily through the categories from philosophy to humor—and he is, or ought to be, equally annoyed if either of them fails to give him the *literary* thrill—the thrill of good words—on top of philosophical knowledge or hilarious entertainment.

JACQUES BARZUN

When Lewis W. Beck was 14 years old, his sister gave him a copy of Will Durant's *The Story of Philosophy*. Sixty years later, as a faculty member at the University of Rochester, he spoke of her gift. "I cannot say how much I learned from and how much I delighted in that book—I still remember it with pleasure. What was most important to me was discovering that there had been others before me who had had the kind of thoughts and asked the kind of questions that had bothered me . . . What I had thought an idiosyncrasy to be hidden from others turned out to be a healthy and traditional exercise of thought. I discovered I was not alone, and not the first to ask questions most of my fellows thought silly."

LEWIS W. BECK

A book is good company. It is full of conversation without loquacity.

Where is human nature so weak as in a bookstore?

HENRY WARD BEECHER

Child! Do not throw this book about!
Refrain from the unholy pleasure
Of cutting all the pictures out!
Preserve it as your chiefest treasure.

HILAIRE BELLOC

Books and harlots have their quarrels in public.

WALTER BENJAMIN

Biography is all about cutting people down to size.

ALAN BENNETT

Books are the compasses and telescopes and sextants and charts which other men have prepared to help us navigate the dangerous seas of human life.

JESSE LEE BENNETT

What is required for a child to be eager to learn to read is not knowledge about reading's practical usefulness, but a fervent belief that being able to read will open to him a world of wonderful experiences, permit him to shed his ignorance, understand the world, and become master of his fate.

A child who is made to read: "Nan had a pad. Nan had a tan pad. Dan ran. Dan ran to the pad . . ." and worse nonsense, does not receive the impression that he is being guided toward becoming literate, because what he is being made to read is obviously not literature. It is not that children do not enjoy playing with words; they love making up words, including nonsense words and rhymes, and revel in their newly gained abilities in doing so. But for such word play to remain enjoyable, it must not be made into a chore, for then all the pleasure goes out of it, and with it out of reading.

Morality is not the issue in [fairy] tales, but rather, assurance that one can succeed . . . More can be learned from them about the inner problems of human beings and of the right solutions to their predicaments in any society than from any other type of story within a child's comprehension.

BRUNO BETTELHEIM

Once as a boy of twelve I was emboldened to search for some books in Leipzig's Municipal Library. To be admitted to its august precincts as a regular user, one needed pledges from three citizens of high standing. After securing these I presented my "want list" to the librarian. Like a dragon protecting his holy grail he viewed me critically, then blurted out with all the friendliness of a drill sergeant: "Come back in three days and we will show you what we have found." No wonder that, by contrast, I was startled upon my arrival in America to find its libraries groaning with books liberally available to all citizens, with no questions asked.

OTTO L. BETTMANN

The only real use of books is to make a person think for himself. If a book will not set one to thinking, it is not worth shelf room.

ALEPH BEY

Ambrose Bierce, author of *The Devil's Dictionary*, wrote the shortest, most lethal book review on record: "The covers of this book are too far apart."

AMBROSE BIERCE

There is a metaphysics of reading that has to do with a great deal more than any simple broadening of the mind. Rather, it involves a change of state and inner orientation, and if we contemplate the reading process in this light we can hardly get away from introducing the word *soul* (or something very like it) into the conversation.

SVEN BIRKERTS

Of all the odd crazes, the craze to be forever reading new books is one of the oddest.

An ordinary man . . . can surround himself with two thousand books . . . and thenceforward have at least one place in the world in which it is possible to be happy.

AUGUSTINE BIRRELL

If you never read a book from cover to cover in one sitting because it's too exciting to put down, you never really learn to read fluently. For so many students, reading is a painful matter of lurching along from word to word, from sentence to sentence, missing the meaning of paragraphs, let alone the chapter, let alone the book.

MARYLAINE BLOCK

When I was little, maybe eight or nine, the books that made an enormous impression on me, and didn't fade, were *The Scarlet Pimpernel*, *A Tale of Two Cities*, and all of the Superman comic books. They all involve the same idea, which is someone who is ineffective and foppish on the surface but powerful and effective and mysterious and unstoppable in secret . . . they encouraged me to develop the notion that you might appear one way but really be another.

AMY BLOOM

We read, frequently if unknowingly, in quest of a mind more original than our own.

My favorite guide to reading would be the critical writings of William Hazlitt and Samuel Johnson and Emerson, who are the critics in the English language who have most influenced me. I don't know anything better than *The Characters of Shakespeare's Plays* by Hazlitt.

We read deeply for varied reasons, most of them familiar: that we cannot know enough people profoundly enough; that we need to know ourselves better; that we require knowledge, not just of self and others, but of the way things are.

HAROLD BLOOM

A wonderful thing about a book, in contrast to a computer screen, is that you can take it to bed with you.

Best sellerism is the star system of the book world. A "best seller" is a celebrity among books. It is a book primarily (sometimes exclusively) known for its well-knownness.

DANIEL J. BOORSTIN

My father gave me free run of his library. When I think of my boyhood, I think of the books I read.

I believe books will never disappear. It is impossible for it to happen. Of all mankind's diverse tools, undoubtedly the most astonishing are his books . . . If books were to disappear, history would disappear. So would men.

JORGE LUIS BORGES

He read, as he did most things, violently; he had a particular facility for seizing at once what was valuable in any book, without submitting to the labour of perusing it from the beginning to the end. He got at the substance of a book directly, tearing out the heart of it. At times he kept a book in readiness for when he should finish the other, resembling a dog who holds a bone in his paws in reserve, while he eats something else which has been thrown to him.

JAMES BOSWELL, describing the reading
habits of Dr. Samuel Johnson

A conventional good read is usually a bad read, a relaxing bath in what we know already. A true good read is surely an act of innovative creation in which we, the readers, become conspirators.

MALCOLM BRADBURY

You don't have to burn books to destroy a culture. Just get people to stop reading them.

RAY BRADBURY

We should be grateful for rotten reviews. While nobody wants to read only what the times approve, we cannot read everything, and some books are so bad, such complete wastes of our finite spans of attention (no matter how well-known the writers that produced them), that the need for some system to winnow them out is self-evident.

ANTHONY BRANDT

> Of splendid books I own no end,
> But few that I can comprehend.
>
> SEBASTIAN BRANT

Some books make me want to go adventuring; others feel that they have saved me the trouble.

The closest you will ever come in this life to an orderly universe is a good library.

ASHLEIGH BRILLIANT

Reading is important. Read between the lines—don't swallow everything.

GWENDOLYN BROOKS

The great threat to the young and pure in heart is not what they read but what they don't read.

In the march up to the heights of fame, there comes a spot close to the summit in which man reads nothing but detective stories.

HEYWOOD BROUN

No one can be called friendless who has God and the companionship of good books.

At painful times, when composition is impossible and reading is not enough, grammars and dictionaries are excellent for distraction.

ELIZABETH BARRETT BROWNING

The contents of someone's bookcase are part of his history, like an ancestral portrait.

ANATOLE BROYARD

Where a book raises your spirit, and inspires you with noble and courageous feelings, seek for no other rule to judge the event by; it is good and made by a good workman.

JEAN DE LA BRUYERE

The book that made the biggest impression on me was *The Catcher in the Rye*. The reason it impressed me was that I identified with Holden Caulfield. He worked one side of the street and I worked the other. It's a classic, and one which will stay with me forever and ever.

ART BUCHWALD

Children are made readers on the laps of their parents.

EMILIE BUCHWALD

Reading about imaginary characters is the greatest pleasure in the world. Or the second greatest.

ANTHONY BURGESS

Through and through th' inspired leaves,
Ye maggots, make your windings;
But O, respect his lordship's taste,
And spare his golden bindings!

ROBERT BURNS

I read books like mad, but I am careful not to let anything I read influence me.

MICHAEL CAINE

A classic is a book that has never finished saying what it has to say.

Who are we, who is each one of us, if not a combination of experiences, information, books we have read, things imagined? Each life is an encyclopedia, a library, an inventory of objects, a series of styles, and everything can be constantly shuffled and reordered in every way conceivable.

ITALO CALVINO

A well-written life is almost as rare as a well-spent one.

The best effect of any book is that it excites the reader to self activity.

THOMAS CARLYLE

There is not such a cradle of democracy upon the earth as the Free Public Library, this republic of letters, where neither rank, office, nor wealth receives the slightest consideration.

It was from my own early experience that I decided there was no use to which money could be applied so productive of good to boys and girls who have good within them and ability and ambition to develop it as the founding of a public library.

ANDREW CARNEGIE

Alice was beginning to get very tired of sitting by her sister on the bank, and of having nothing to do. Once or twice she had peeped into the book her sister was reading, but it had no pictures or conversations in it, "and what is the use of a book," thought Alice, "without pictures or conversations?"

LEWIS CARROLL — opening lines
of *Alice's Adventures in Wonderland*

"Of course you know your ABC?" said the Red Queen.
"To be sure I do," said Alice.
"So do I," the White Queen whispered. "We'll often say it over together, dear. And I'll tell you a secret — I can read words of one letter! Isn't *that* grand? However, don't be discouraged. You'll come to it in time."

LEWIS CARROLL — *Through the Looking-Glass*

I'm 30 years old but I read at the 34-year-old level.

DANA CARVEY

Reading is a pleasure of the mind, which means that it is a little like sport: your eagerness and knowledge and quickness count for something. The fun of reading is not that something is told you, but that you stretch your mind. Your own imagination works along with the author's, or even goes beyond his. Your experience, compared with his, yields the same or different conclusions, and your ideas develop as you understand his.

BENNETT CERF

The ideal mystery is the one you would read if the end was missing.

RAYMOND CHANDLER

In the best books, great men talk to us, give us their most precious thoughts, and pour their souls into ours.

Let every man, if possible, gather some good books under his roof, and obtain access for himself and family to some social library. Almost any luxury should be sacrificed to this.

WILLIAM ELLERY CHANNING

Let blockheads read what blockheads write.

LORD CHESTERFIELD

There is a great deal of difference between the eager man who wants to read a book and the tired man who wants a book to read.

The *Iliad* is great because all of life is a battle; the *Odyssey* is great because all of life is a journey; the book of Job is great because all of life is a riddle.

G. K. Chesterton, English journalist and author, was a friend of George Bernard Shaw, H. G. Wells, and Hilaire Belloc. He is widely known as writer of the Father Brown stories of detection. An interviewer once asked Chesterton what book he would like to have with him if he were marooned on a desert island. A volume of Shakespeare? A Bible? Chesterton shook his head. He'd much prefer, he said, *Thomas's Guide to Practical Shipbuilding*.

G. K. CHESTERTON

I've found that lining the walls of our 1884 vintage brick house with bookcases packed with the 1,700-plus volumes of my library has made a significant difference in keeping the old place warm in winter and cool in summer.

RON CHIDESTER

After three days without reading, talk becomes flavorless.

CHINESE PROVERB

If you cannot read all your books, at any rate handle, or as it were, fondle them—peer into them, let them fall open where they will, read from the first sentence that arrests the eye, set them back on the shelves with your own hands, arrange them on your own plan so that you at least know where they are. Let them be your friends; let them at any rate be your acquaintances.

WINSTON CHURCHILL

To add a library to a house is to give that house a soul.

MARCUS TULLIUS CICERO

I like being around books. It makes me feel civilized. The only way to do all the things you'd like to do is to read.

TOM CLANCY

I am sure I read every book of fairy tales in our branch library, with one complaint—all that long, golden hair. Never mind— my short brown hair became long and golden as I read and when I grew up I would write a book about a brown-haired girl to even things up.

BEVERLY CLEARY

Books never annoy; they cost little, and they are always at hand, and ready at your call.

WILLIAM COBBETT

There are four kinds of readers. The first is like the hour-glass; and their reading being as the sand, it runs in and runs out, and leaves not a vestige behind. A second is like the sponge, which imbibes everything, and returns it in nearly the same state, only a little dirtier. A third is like a jelly-bag, allowing all that is pure to pass away, and retaining only the refuse and dregs. And the fourth is like the slaves in the diamond mines of Golconda, who, casting aside all that is worthless, retain only pure gems.

SAMUEL TAYLOR COLERIDGE

It is poor traveling that is only to arrive, and it is poor reading that is only to find out how the book ends.

ARTHUR W. COLTON

Some read to think, these are rare; some to write, these are common; and some read to talk, and these form the great majority.

CHARLES CALEB COLTON

The best of my education has come from the public library . . . my tuition fee is a bus fare and once in a while, five cents for an overdue book. You don't need to know very much to start with, if you know the way to the public library.

LESLEY CONGER

Literature is the art of writing something that will be read twice.

CYRIL CONNOLLY

Of all the inanimate objects, of all of man's creations, books are the nearest to us, for they contain our very thought, our ambitions, our indignations, our fidelity to truth, and our persistent leaning towards error.

JOSEPH CONRAD

A library is the delivery room for the birth of ideas, a place where history comes to life.

The trouble with contemporary novels is that they are full of people not worth knowing. The characters slide in and out of the mind with hardly a ripple.

NORMAN COUSINS

> May I a small house and large garden have;
> And a few friends, and many books, both true,
> Both wise, and both delightful too!

ABRAHAM COWLEY

Every book salesman is an advance agent for culture and for better citizenship, for education and for the spread of intelligence.

DR. FRANK CRANE

Fast reading is supposed to save time. Sprinting through a live oak grove saves time, too, but sometimes it's pleasanter to stroll.

The grownups of that time frowned on the western novels of Zane Grey as too rough and too violent. It was felt that he might lead the nation's youth into uncouth habits such as carrying their pistols in a holster instead of the hip pocket, where they belonged. The best thing that anybody could say about Zane Grey was that none of his heroes used tobacco.

PAUL CRUME

Sartor Resartus is simply unreadable, and for me that always sort of spoils a book.

WILL CUPPY

Reading has a history. It was not always and everywhere the same. We may think of it as a straightforward process of lifting information from a page; but if we considered it further, we would agree that information must be sifted, sorted, and interpreted . . . As our ancestors lived in different mental worlds, they must have read differently, and the history of reading could be as complex as the history of thinking.

ROBERT DARNTON

The reader cannot create. That has been done for him by the

author. The reader can only interpret, giving the author a fair chance to make his impression.

When we read, we must always be aware of the mind that lies behind the book. Not that we may be wholly persuaded by it, or that we should have no minds of our own, but that we may share it and be shown new meanings by it.

Our grandparents used to say that we must eat a peck of dirt before we die, and they were right. And you must read a lot of rubbish before you die, as well, because an exclusive diet of masterpieces will give you spiritual dyspepsia. How do you know that a mountain peak is glorious if you have never scrambled through a dirty valley? How do you know that your gourmet meal is perfect in its kind if you have never eaten a roadside hot dog?

We can read any way we please. When I was a boy, and was known to be fond of reading, many patronizing adults assured me that there was nothing I liked better than to "curl up with a book." I despised them. I have never curled. My physique is not formed for it. It is a matter of legend that Abraham Lincoln read lying on his stomach in front of the fire; you should try that in order to understand the extraordinary indifference to physical comfort that Lincoln possessed.

I have never scorned newspapers as many people do. I have long been mindful of the words of Henrik Ibsen, who, when asked what he read, replied that he read only the Bible and the daily papers, and there he found everything he needed. And indeed, if you read the newspapers perceptively, you will find the great themes of the Bible, of Homer, of Shakespeare, repeated again and again. When I was a teacher I used to tell my students that if they thought the plot of *Othello* farfetched, they had only to read the *Toronto Globe and Mail* any Monday morning to find that the plot had been recreated and reenacted in some suburb over the weekend.

If you don't like the book, you do not have to read it. Put it aside and read something you do like, because there is no reason at all why you should read what bores you during your serious reading time. You have to read enough boring stuff in the ordinary way of life without extending the borders of ennui. But if you do like the book, if it engages you seriously, do not rush at it. Read it at the pace when you can pronounce and hear every word in your own head. Read eloquently.

ROBERTSON DAVIES

The world of books is the most remarkable creation of man. Nothing else that he builds ever lasts. Monuments fall; nations perish; civilizations grow old and die out; and, after an era of darkness, new races build others. But in the world of books are volumes that have seen this happen again and again, and yet live on, still young, still as fresh as the day they were written, still telling men's hearts of the hearts of men centuries dead.

CLARENCE DAY

Reading all the good books is like a conversation with the finest people of past centuries.

RENÉ DESCARTES

Every novel should have a beginning, a muddle, and an end.

PETER DE VRIES

There are books of which the backs and covers are by far the best part.

CHARLES DICKENS

I don't often reread books, except poetry. And when I do get a yen to go back to something, either I can't find it or I find the print too small. Everything I bought in college is in the second category, everything I want to lend or quote from in the first. So I have to go buy a new copy, but all the new copies have small print, too.

MARGARET DIEHL

Why are we reading, if not in hope that the writer will magnify and dramatize our days, will illuminate and inspire us with wisdom, courage, and the hope of meaningfulness, and press upon our minds the deepest mysteries, so we may feel again their majesty and power?

ANNIE DILLARD

There is more treasure in books than in all the pirates' loot on Treasure Island . . . and best of all, you can enjoy these riches every day of your life.

WALT DISNEY

"Many thanks. I shall lose no time reading it."

BENJAMIN DISRAELI, on receiving an unsolicited manuscript

Bibliomania, or the collecting of an enormous heap of books without intelligent curiosity, has, since libraries existed, infected weak minds, who imagine that they themselves acquire knowledge when they keep it on their shelves.

ISAAC D'ISRAELI

Reading great books whets but never slakes the thirst for greatness.

J. FRANK DOBIE

Children have a lot more to worry about from the parents who raised them than from the books they read.

E. L. DOCTOROW

Summers lasted forever when I was growing up in Texas. They were hot and they were muggy and they were very still—unless I happened to be sprawled belly-down on the linoleum with an oscillating fan tickling my toes and a Nancy Drew mystery under my nose. To my mind, that was as close to heaven as a Houston girl could get.

DIANNE DONOVAN

My mother and father were illiterate immigrants from Russia. When I was a child they were constantly amazed that I could go to a building and take a book on any subject. They couldn't believe this access to knowledge we have here in America. They couldn't believe that it was free.

KIRK DOUGLAS

A man should keep his little brain attic stocked with all the furniture that he is likely to use, and the rest he can put away in the lumber room of his library, where he can get at it if he wants it.

SIR ARTHUR CONAN DOYLE

I enjoy reading biographies because I want to know about the people who messed up the world.

MARIE DRESSLER

Born to a house without books, I now live in a library. Twice I've had to move because I needed more room for all the books. At night we hear the beams and foundations shift under the weight of the books . . . Painful as it is, I've started donating books. We are out of space and can't afford to move. Besides, no mover would have us.

BOB EDWARDS

Books are the quietest and most constant of friends; they are the most accessible and wisest of counselors, and the most patient of teachers.

CHARLES W. ELIOT

I read much of the night, and go south in the winter.

T. S. ELIOT

What one reads becomes part of what one sees and feels.

RALPH ELLISON

If we encounter a man of rare intellect, we should ask him what books he reads.

What can we see, read, acquire, but ourselves? Take the book, my friend, and read your eyes out, you will never find there what I find.

In reading there is a sort of half-and-half mixture. The book must be good, but the reader must also be active.

RALPH WALDO EMERSON

You can't tell a book by its cover.

ENGLISH PROVERB

I always read the last page of a book first, so that if I die before I finish I'll know how it turned out.

NORA EPHRON

New York probably offers more good reasons to avert one's eyes than any other city in America, and where better to avert them than into a book? To this day, although long removed from New York, I still usually walk about with a book in hand, and I keep a book or two in my car, often getting in a quick paragraph at a stop light. If you happen to be behind me, please don't honk when the light turns green, for I could be coming to the end of a paragraph.

Lots of people—I am among them—read while watching television, sometimes during commercials or through the more trivial news items or awaiting a weather report or sport scores. Reading while watching a baseball game on television is especially fine and, given light reading, is easily brought off with the help of the instant replay.

JOSEPH EPSTEIN

When I get a little money, I buy books; and if there is any left, I buy food and clothes.

A little before you sleep, read something that is exquisite and worth remembering; and when you awake in the morning, call yourself to an account for it.

DESIDERIUS ERASMUS

There is no reader so parochial as the one who reads this morning's books. Books are not rolls, to be devoured only when they are hot and fresh. A good book retains its interior heat and will warm a generation yet unborn.

Civilized man is a reader. Irrevocably he would appear to be committed to the scanning of small black marks on plane surfaces. It is, when you come to think it over, an odd gesture, like the movement the camera catches of the heads of a tennis audience. But there it is—we are readers, and it's too late to change.

CLIFTON FADIMAN

The books I read are the ones I knew and loved when I was a young man and to which I return as you do to friends: the Old Testament, Dickens, Conrad, Cervantes—*Don Quixote*. I read that every year, as some do the Bible . . . I've read these books so often that I don't always begin at page one and read on to the end. I just read one scene, or about one character just as you'd meet and talk to a friend for a few minutes.

WILLIAM FAULKNER

The more our acquaintance with good books increases, the smaller becomes the circle of people whose company is to our taste.

LUDWIG FEUERBACH

I once read Flannery O'Connor to find out how to write, but in the end she gave me much more than that. She showed me how to live.

HAROLD FICKETT

Women are by nature fickle, and so are men . . . Not so with books, for books cannot change. A thousand years hence they are what you find them today, speaking the same words, holding forth the same comfort.

EUGENE FIELD

My interest began as an interest in reading, which then was

translated into an interest in writing . . . I can remember a Sunday school prize or something when I was about eleven years old; I won a copy of *David Copperfield*. Up to that time I'd read the Bobbsey Twins and then Tom Swift and the Rover Boys and Tarzan, but since I got this as a prize, I decided I should read it. I found a world that was realer than the world I lived in, unlike these Tarzan and other books. I knew David Copperfield better than anybody I knew in the real world, including myself.

SHELBY FOOTE

One always tends to overpraise a long book because one has got through it.

Books have to be read. It is the only way of discovering what they contain. A few savage tribes eat them, but reading is the only method of assimilation revealed to the West.

E. M. FORSTER

Never lend books, for no one ever returns them. The only books I have in my library are books that other folk have lent me.

ANATOLE FRANCE

I would advise you to read with a pen in your hand, and enter in a little book short hints of what you find that is curious or that might be useful; for this will be the best method of imprinting such particulars in your memory, where they will be ready on some future occasion to adorn and improve your conversation.

Often I sat up in my room reading the greatest part of the night, when a book was borrowed in the evening and had to be returned early in the morning, lest it should be missed or wanted.

BENJAMIN FRANKLIN

Thou mayest as well expect to grow stronger by always eating, as wiser by always reading. Too much overcharges Nature, and turns more into disease than nourishment. 'Tis thought and digestion which makes books serviceable, and give health and vigor to the mind.

THOMAS FULLER

Generally speaking, people are plagued with problems that they are unable to solve. To escape them they pick up a detective story, become completely absorbed, help bring the investigation to a successful conclusion, switch off the light and go to sleep.

ERLE STANLEY GARDNER

If the book had been invented after the laptop computer, it would have been hailed as a great breakthrough.

NEIL GERSHENFIELD

I think nine times out of ten a collaborator, a ghostwriter, or call it what you will, probably deserves to have his or her name on the cover of the book just in recognition for all the work. But sometimes when you're dealing with these great historical figures, it's a good idea to say, "It's your book. I'm not going to appear with you on Mount Rushmore. It's not the Gettysburg Address by Abraham Lincoln with Roger Gittines."

ROGER GITTINES

Books are a delightful society. If you go into a room and find it full of books—even without taking them from the shelves—they seem to speak to you, to bid you welcome. They seem to tell you that they have got something inside their covers that will be good for you, and that they are willing and desirous to impart to you. Value them much.

WILLIAM GLADSTONE

The ancient writers were close observers of humanity who help us better understand ourselves and the need for human beings to live ethically and with dignity.

Sometimes we stand in a used bookstore with a volume in our

hand and marvel over the foolishness of someone who would rid themselves of such a glorious treasure. "How could they?" we mutter to ourselves as we smile over our own wisdom.

Books provide the most helpful of road maps for (an) inner journey. They show us the tracks of fellow travelers, footprints left by earlier pilgrims who have trod the path that stretches before us. Their luminosity helps to light our way. As we read we realize that we are not alone.

TERRY W. GLASPEY

The second part of the history of the world and the arts begins with the invention of printing.

Some books seem to have been written, not to teach us anything, but to let us know that the author has known something.

JOHANN WOLFGANG VON GOETHE

A book may be amusing with numerous errors, or it may be very dull without a single absurdity.

The first time I read an excellent book, it is for me just as if I had gained a new friend. When I read over a book I have perused before, it resembles the meeting with an old one.

OLIVER GOLDSMITH

We used to be a closed society ideologically—a very closed, controlled society. And that meant that even well-educated people did not get a chance to read many of the books of Russian philosophers because our ideologues did not like those philosophers. But when we began perestroika, we very quickly published thirty volumes of all the philosophers of pre-revolutionary Russia. And I have those volumes, and I read a lot by them. They were great minds: Ilian, Solovyov, Perdiyev. They said a great deal of what today we are only rehashing. So sometimes we are reinventing the wheel. That is our problem. We reinvent the wheel. We sometimes think as though there were no thinkers before us, and that can be tragic. We really have to go back to those thinkers and writers.

MIKHAIL GORBACHEV

The remarkable thing about Shakespeare is that he is really very good, in spite of all the people who say he is very good.

ROBERT GRAVES

Books become as familiar and necessary as old friends. Each change in them, brought about by much handling and by accident, only endears them more. They are an extension of oneself.

CHARLOTTE GRAY

I've never been much on folklore—it has a perverse way of jumping from one region to another by merely changing local names. Fun to read, but hard to lay much store by.

A. C. GREENE

The chief reason that so many of the great classics seem to speak directly to us is that the authors were consciously trying to reach us, or at least people with an astonishing resemblance to us.

MARTIN W. GROSS

It is the writer's fault, not the reader's, if the reader puts down the book.

DAVID HALBERSTAM

There are ten thousand books in my library, and it will keep growing until I die. This has exasperated my daughters, amused my friends, and baffled my accountant. If I had not picked up this habit in the library long ago, I would have more money in the bank today; I would not be richer.

PETE HAMILL

I do love secondhand books that open to the page some previous owner read oftenest.

HELEN HANFF

The great gift is the passion for reading. It is cheap, it consoles, it distracts, it excites. It gives you knowledge of the world and experience of a wide kind. It is moral illumination.

ELIZABETH HARDWICK

In a very real sense, people who have read good literature have lived more than people who cannot or will not read. It is not true that we can have only one life to live. If we can read, we can live as many lives and as many kinds of lives as we wish.

S. I. HAYAKAWA

Make it a rule never to read at mealtime, not in company when there is (even the most trivial) conversation going on, nor ever to let your eagerness to learn encroach upon your play-hours. Books are but one inlet of knowledge; and the pores of the mind, like those of the body, should be left open to all impressions.

WILLIAM HAZLITT

To those with ears to hear, libraries are really very noisy places. On their shelves we hear the captured voices of the centuries-old conversation that makes up our civilization.

TIMOTHY HEALY

Your family sees you as a lazy lump lying on the couch, propping a book up on your stomach, never realizing that you are in the middle of an African safari that has just been charged by elephants, or in the drawing room of a large English country house interrogating the butler about the body discovered on the Aubusson carpet.

CYNTHIA HEIMEL

Research demonstrates that people who do not use their brains will lose some of their mental capacity as they grow older. By perpetually engaging one's mind through reading, innovative people can help sustain their mental capacity. Embrace the motto "Use it or lose it!"

HOWARD G. HENDRICKS

Without words, without writing, and without books there would be no history, there could be no concept of humanity.

HERMANN HESSE

The foolishest book is a kind of leaky boat on a sea of wisdom. Some of the wisdom will get in somehow.

If I were a prince, I would hire . . . a person whose sole business should be to read day and night, and talk to me whenever I wanted him to.

OLIVER WENDELL HOLMES

When I get hold of a book I particularly admire, I am so enthusiastic that I loan it to someone who never brings it back.

EDGAR W. HOWE

Everything comes to him who waits, except a loaned book.

MCKINNEY HUBBARD

To completely analyze what we do when we read would almost be the acme to a psychologist's achievements, for it would be to describe very many of the most intricate workings of the human mind.

E. B. HUEY

This is a book to take with you on a morning's bird-watching session or a night of stargazing. Pack it with your picnic on a mountain bike, tote it along for beach reading. Press a wildflower between its pages, or find a russet-colored autumn leaf for your bookmark. Read, think, and meditate upon nature—after all, it's the human thing to do.

HOLLY HUGHES
from introduction to *Meditations on the Earth*

It is from books that wise men derive consolation in the troubles of life.

VICTOR HUGO

Every man who knows how to read has it in his power to magnify himself, to multiply the ways in which he exists, to make his life full, significant, and interesting.

ALDOUS HUXLEY

Never refuse to lend books to anyone who cannot afford to purchase them, but lend books only to those who can be trusted to return them.

JUDAH IBN-TIBBON

There is no worse robber than a bad book.

ITALIAN PROVERB

I taught myself to read by comparing the words in the *TV Guide* to the names the announcers spoke. The first words I could read were "I," "love," and "Lucy."

MITCHELL IVERS

All guidance in reading should be treated, if not with suspicion, at least with care.

The time to read is any time. No apparatus, no appointment of time and place is necessary. It is the only art which can be practiced at any hour of the day or night, whenever the time and inclination comes, that is your time for reading; in joy or sorrow, health or illness.

HOLBROOK JACKSON

Detective stories help reassure us in the belief that the universe, underneath it all, is rational. They're small celebrations of order and reason in an increasingly disordered world.

P. D. JAMES

If you believe everything you read, better not read.

JAPANESE PROVERB

From candlelight to early bedtime, I read.

Were it left to me to decide whether we should have a government without newspapers, or newspapers without a government, I should not hesitate a moment to prefer the latter. But I should mean that every man should receive those papers and be capable of reading them.

THOMAS JEFFERSON

Quotation is the highest compliment you can pay to an author.

The only end of writing is to enable readers better to enjoy life or better to endure it.

One advantage there certainly is in quotation: that if the authors cited be good, there is at least so much worth reading in the book of him who quotes them.

DR. SAMUEL JOHNSON

One problem with developing speed-reading skills is that by the time you realize a book is boring, you've already finished it.

FRANKLIN P. JONES

A great library is the most important element in the formation of a great university.

DAVID STARR JORDAN

A reader finds little in a book save what he puts there. But in a great book he finds space to put many things.

JOSEPH JOUBERT

I have good reason to be content for, thank God, I can read and perhaps understand Shakespeare to his depths.

JOHN KEATS

As a former English major I am a sitting duck for gift books, and in the past few years I've gotten Dickens, Thackeray, Smollett, Richardson, Emerson, Keats, Boswell, and the Brontës, all of them Great, none of them ever read by me, all of them now on my shelf, looking at me and making me feel guilty.

GARRISON KEILLOR

I have sought for happiness everywhere, but I have found it nowhere except in a little corner with a little book.

If he shall not lose his reward who gives a cup of cold water to his thirsty neighbor, what will not be the reward of those who by putting books into the hands of those neighbors, open to them the fountains of eternal life?

THOMAS A KEMPIS

The librarian gave Geordie *Mother Goose's Nursery Rhymes*. Geordie read it from cover to cover, and when I asked him how he liked it he said, "It's nowt but a pack of lies."

GERALD KERSH

One of the books I really loved, at the fairly advanced age of fourteen, was Louisa May Alcott's *Little Women*. I was staying at the time at my grandmother's house, with a lot of cousins around, and I didn't want anyone to know—so I kept it secret like a piece of pornography. I found it absolutely captivating.

TRACY KIDDER

Reading together puts you and your children in touch with one of the great civilizing traditions of the human race. All the great cultures of the past preferred to express their most serious thought through stories.The wonder of it is that we can share in many of those same stories today. They have survived because the truths they tell are timeless.

WILLIAM KILPATRICK

Once I knew how to read, I loved it so much that I read everything in front of me. I read the Bible and for my seventh birthday my mother gave me a copy of the *Concise Oxford English Dictionary*. Since I had nothing else but the Bible to read, I also read the dictionary. How I loved it! But somehow, somewhere, I lost it, and as if to make up for that loss, I am forever buying a dictionary and comparing definitions and meanings.

JAMAICA KINCAID

I don't want to just mess with your head. I want to mess with your life. I want you to miss appointments, burn dinner, skip your homework. I want you to tell your wife to take that moonlight stroll on the beach at Waikiki with the resort tennis pro while you read a few more chapters.

STEPHEN KING

It is possible that our reading, if so be we read wisely, may save us to a certain extent from some of the serious forms of trouble; or if we get into trouble, as we most certainly shall, may teach us how to come out of it decently.

RUDYARD KIPLING

When it comes to most important events and almost all lives, the truth will not be found in one book but from reading many books, and trying to form, from many different sources, one's own independent judgment. The existence of the Internet, with its ability to produce instant news and unlimited amounts of individual opinions, is going to make this exercise of judgment even more important, and harder, than it is now.

MICHAEL KORDA

Those who do not develop the pleasure reading habit simply don't have a chance—they will have a very difficult time reading and writing at a level high enough to deal with the demands of today's world.

Reading enhances literary development leading to an uncontroversial conclusion: reading is good for you. Reading is the only way we become good readers, develop a good writing style, an adequate vocabulary, advanced grammar, and the only way we become good spellers.

STEPHEN KRASHEN

I thrive on reading because it stimulates me. The added bonus is that I can stimulate others with what I have read. I enjoy that process—it's like cross-pollination.

MICHAEL KRASNY

Only three things are necessary to make life happy: the blessing of God, books, and a friend.

JEAN BAPTISTE LACORDAIRE

A book reads the better which is our own, and has been so long known to us that we know the topography of its blots and dog's-ears, and can trace the dirt in it to having read it at tea with buttered muffins, or over a pipe, which I think is the maximum.

CHARLES LAMB

Nothing is pleasanter than exploring a library.

WALLACE S. LANDOR

A common complaint is that children's books, especially high-quality picture-books, cost so much. All I can say is that they cost less than a dinner out, or a new pair of jeans. The books I read as a child transformed me, gave meaning and perspective to my experiences, and helped to mould whatever imaginative, intellectual or creative strengths I can lay claim to now. No doll or game had that impact on me, no pair of jeans ever changed my life.

MICHELLE LANDSBERG

Mr. Cobb took me into his library and showed me his books, of which he has a complete set.

RING LARDNER

The greatest thrill I have ever had is to see the joy in a person's face when he first learns to read. I would rather see that than to eat.

A literate person is not only an illiterate person who has learned to read and write, he is another person. He is different.

To promote literacy is to change man's conscience by changing his relation to his environment. It is an undertaking on the same plane as the recognition and incarnation of fundamental human rights.

DR. FRANK LAUBACH

Magazines all too frequently lead to books and should be regarded as the heavy petting of literature.

FRAN LEBOWITZ

The man who has taught the ABCs to his pupils has accomplished a greater deed than a general who has won a battle.

GOTTFRIED LEIBNIZ

Reading and writing are inexorably intertwined. Children who love to read acquire a sense of written language that spills over into their writing. Children who write stories and poems and memoirs read with a much greater alertness and insight. They start to notice how an author is setting a scene, or describing a character, or using imagery.

I do think that if you want your children to have a joyous, easy relationship with books—and with learning in general—you have to tolerate a certain amount of disorder. You have to let your kids have some control over their environment—and that will probably mean piles of magazines here, lots of sporting goods over there . . . Just keep saying to yourself: "In eighteen years they'll go away to college."

MARY LEONHARDT

You can't get a cup of tea large enough or a book long enough to suit me.

Those who read poetry to improve their minds will never improve their minds by reading poetry, for the true enjoyments must be spontaneous.

We can never know that a piece of writing is bad unless we

have begun by trying to read it as if it was very good and ended by discovering that we were paying the author an undeserved compliment.

The great blessing of my youth was that I grew up in a world of cheap and abundant books.

Our most esteemed poets and critics are read by our most esteemed critics and poets (who usually don't like them much) and nobody else takes any notice. An increasing number of highly literate people simply ignore what the "Highbrows" are doing. It says nothing to them. The Highbrows in return ignore or insult them.

An unliterary man may be defined as one who reads books once only. There is hope for a man who has never read Malory or Boswell or *Tristram Shandy* or Shakespeare's *Sonnets*; but what can you do with a man who says he "has read" them, meaning he has read them once, and thinks that settles the matter?

The great thing is to be always reading but not to get bored—treat it not like work, more as a vice! Your book bill ought to be your biggest extravagance.

In his autobiography *Surprised by Joy*, C. S. Lewis recalled his parents sitting in their comfortable chairs every evening, engrossed in the books they were reading. During his childhood, Lewis said, he was surrounded by books: "There were books in the study, books in the drawing room, books in the cloakroom, books (two deep) in the great bookcase on the landing, books in a bedroom, books piled high as my shoulder in the cistern attic, books of all kinds reflecting every transient stage of my parents' interest, books readable and unreadable, books suitable for a child and books most emphatically not. Nothing was forbidden me. In the seemingly endless rainy afternoons I took volume after volume down from the shelves. I had always the same certainty of finding a book that was new to me as a man who walks into a field has of finding a new blade of grass."

C. S. LEWIS

When audiences come to see us authors lecture, it is largely in the hope that we'll be funnier to look at than to read.

SINCLAIR LEWIS

I regard reviews as a kind of infant's disease to which newborn books are subject.

It would be a good idea if children would write books for older people, now that everyone is writing books for children.

Desultory reading has always been my greatest pleasure.

The ancients wrote at a time when the great art of writing badly had not yet been invented. In those days, to write at all meant to write well.

G. C. LICHTENBERG

The things I want to know are in books. My best friend is the man who will give me a book I have not read.

A capacity and taste for reading gives access to whatever has already been discovered by others.

ABRAHAM LINCOLN

Reading furnishes the mind only with materials of knowledge. It is thinking that makes what we read ours.

JOHN LOCKE

This is a volume which it will be found exceedingly easy to leave alone.

FREDERICK LOCKE-LAMPSON

Literature is mostly about having sex and not much about having children. Life is the other way around.

DAVID LODGE

If we could get our parents to read to their preschool children fifteen minutes a day, we could revolutionize the schools.

DR. RUTH LOVE

There is the knowledge which reading can convey more swiftly and surely than whole armies of sages in the past, or all our multitudinous babblings out of boxes in the present. For one can read faster than anybody can talk. One can skip. One can reread what a first reading left obscure.

The man who reads can become older in experience by three thousand years; if he does not become thereby a little wiser also, the fault must be his. An active mind can develop as constant a hunger for the ideas as the body has for its daily bread. It is not the unhappiest type of mind. And its happiest hunting-ground must be found in books.

F. L. LUCAS

Censorship, like charity, should begin at home; but unlike charity, it should end there.

CLARE BOOTHE LUCE

I thank whatever gods may be that at 73 my taste for reading is undiminished, and another blessing at that age is that you no longer read what you ought to read, but what you want to.

GEORGE LYTTLETON

It was a book to kill time for those who liked it better dead.

ROSE MACAULAY

Books are becoming everything to me. If I had at this moment any choice of life, I would bury myself in one of those immense libraries . . . and never pass a waking hour without a book before me.

THOMAS MACAULAY

The familiar faces of my books welcomed me. I threw myself into my reading chair and gazed around me with pleasure. All my old friends present—there in spirit, ready to talk with me any moment when I was in the mood, making no claim upon my attention when I was not.

GEORGE MACDONALD

. . . the terrible isolation of the nonreader, his life without meaning or substance because he cannot comprehend the world in which he lives.

JOHN D. MACDONALD

How can one not find the time to read? There's no other substitute for finding out about the human condition. You can go to plays and movies and you can travel, but nothing else gives you, in such a concentrated and economical way, both in terms of time and money, the rich exposure to the human condition that reading does. Your soul is very much smaller if you don't read.

ROBERT MACNEIL

I take pleasure in lending a book to one who loves it, takes care of it, and returns it within two weeks.

CHARLES MAJOR

My alma mater was books, a good library . . . I could spend the rest of my life reading, just satisfying my curiosity.

MALCOLM X

The world exists to be put into a book.

STEPHANE MALLARMÉ

Once I had learned to read my letters, I read everything: books, but also notices, advertisements, the small type on the back of tramway tickets, letters tossed into the garbage, weathered newspapers caught under my bench in the park, graffiti, the back covers of magazines held by other readers on the bus. When I found that Cervantes, in his fondness for reading, read "even the torn bits of paper in the street," I knew exactly what urge drove him to this scavenging.

ALBERTO MANGUEL

Resolve to edge in a little reading every day, if it is but a single sentence. If you gain fifteen minutes a day, it will make itself felt at the end of the year.

HORACE MANN

Isn't it a joy—there is hardly a greater one—to find a new book, a living book, and know that it will remain with you while life lasts?

KATHERINE MANSFIELD

In journalism just one fact that is false prejudices the entire work. In contrast, in fiction one single fact that is true gives legitimacy to the entire work.

GABRIEL GARCIA MARQUEZ

Readers are plentiful; thinkers are rare.

HARRIET MARTINEAU

From the moment I picked up your book I was convulsed with laughter. Some day I intend reading it.

Outside of a dog, a book is a man's best friend. Inside of a dog, it's too dark to read.

I find television very educating. Every time someone turns the set on, I go into the other room and read a book.

GROUCHO MARX

I would sooner read a timetable or a catalog than nothing at all. They are much more entertaining than half the novels that are written.

W. SOMERSET MAUGHAM

In literature, as in love, we are astonished at what is chosen by others.

ANDRE MAUROIS

When I walk into a bookstore I feel a physical change, an adrenaline rush, just like other people get when they walk into a gambling casino. I take out my charge card and spend too much money.

MAGGIE MCBRIDE

Oscar Wilde said that he put his genius in his life, and only his talent into his work, but his work is, of course, full of genius. When I was fifteen, I had much of *The Ballad of Reading Gaol* memorized, which did not make me a whole lot of fun at parties.

ELIZABETH MCCRACKEN

Harry Truman was a reader. He was a lifelong reader. I asked Margaret one day, "What would be your father's idea of heaven?" She said, "Oh, that's easy. It would be a good comfortable armchair and a good reading lamp and a stack of new history and biography that he wanted to read." He once said that all readers can't be leaders, but all leaders must be readers.

DAVID MCCULLOUGH

A book that helps a child to form a habit of reading, to make reading one of his deep and continuing needs, is good for him.

RICHARD MCKENNA

Today's young, expanding imaginations are packed with a far more diverse set of characters and stories than mine was at a comparable age. In the forties my only access to the classics would have been through the always pallid Classic Comics. Now the young imagination is apt to be crammed with characters, both old and new. Odysseus and Don Quixote mix with Kermit the Frog, Bert and Ernie, Han Solo and Luke Skywalker—even, soon enough, Bart Simpson and Beavis and Butthead. The story-seeking children of today are far from impoverished.

LARRY MCMURTRY

One smart reader is worth a thousand boneheads.

I read them all, sometimes with shivers of puzzlement and sometimes with delight, but always calling for more. I began to inhabit a world that was two-thirds letterpress and only one-third trees, fields, streets, and people. I acquired round shoulders, spindly shanks, and a despondent view of humanity. I read everything that I could find in English, taking in some of it but boggling most of it.

H. L. MENCKEN

In the unbroken chain of which I am a part, reading breeds writing, which breeds more reading.

As a boy I was saved from a life of ignorance by my little home-town library. As a college student I was educated in the stacks of the Swarthmore library. And as an adult I use libraries daily in my search for the facts and the enlightenment I use in writing my books. In fact, I like libraries so much that I married a librarian.

JAMES MICHENER

Ironically, it was the fertile imagination of a science-fiction writer, Ray Bradbury, that gave root to my maturing understanding of how to get along without the burdensome world at hand . . . Reading Bradbury exposes the reader to the possibility of sudden, mind-expanding experiences, but not only that. His works are also suffused with his wide learning from the classics.

CALVIN MILLER

Though reading may not at first blush seem like an act of creation, to a deep sense it is. Without the enthusiastic reader, who is really the author's counterpart and very often his most secret rival, a book would die.

HENRY MILLER

Show me the books he loves and I shall know the man far better than through mortal friends.

SILAS WEIR MITCHELL

I have only read one book in my life and that is *White Fang*. It's so frightfully good that I've never bothered to read another.

NANCY MITFORD*

*This quotation has also been attributed to Nancy Mitford's father, Lord Redesdale. (See *Nancy Mitford: A Memoir*, by Sir Harold Acton.)

I know of no sentence that can induce such immediate and brazen lying as the one that begins, "Have you read . . ."

WILSON MIZNER

No entertainment is so cheap as reading, nor any pleasure so lasting.

MARY WORTLEY MONTAGU

Study has been for me the sovereign remedy against all the disappointments of life. I have never known any trouble that an hour's reading would not dissipate.

BARON DE MONTESQUIEU

Blessed be the inventor of the alphabet, pen and printing press! Life would be to me in all events a terrible thing without books.

LUCY MAUD MONTGOMERY

A book is the only place where you can examine a fragile thought without breaking it, or explore an explosive idea without fear it will go off in your face.

EDWARD P. MORGAN

A book isn't born until someone reads it.

The bookstore is one of humanity's great engines—one of the greatest instruments of civilization.

Read, every day, something no one else is reading. Think, every day, something no one else is thinking. Do, every day, something no one else would be silly enough to do. It is bad for the mind to be always part of unanimity.

When you sell a man a book, you don't sell him 12 ounces of paper and ink and glue—you sell him a whole new life. Love and friendship and humor and ships at sea by night—there's all heaven and earth in a book, a real book I mean.

The perfect reader . . . broods constantly as to whether he himself, in some happy conjuncture of quick mind and environing silence and the sudden perfect impulse, might have written something like that . . .

CHRISTOPHER MORLEY

I don't believe in children's books. I think after you've read *Kidnapped*, *Treasure Island* and *Huckleberry Finn*, you're ready for anything.

JOHN MORTIMER

A truly great novel is a tale to the simple, a parable to the wise, and a direct revelation of reality to a man who has made it part of his being.

JOHN MIDDLETON MURRY

A good reader is one who has imagination, memory, a dictionary, and some artistic sense.

VLADIMIR NABOKOV

My son should read much history and meditate upon it. It is the only true philosophy.

NAPOLEON

Another book was opened, which is the book of life . . .

NEW TESTAMENT, Revelation 20:12

Librarian to borrower: "It's not a dirty book. It's an *earthy* book, which is a very different thing."

NEW YORKER cartoon caption

As sheer casual reading matter, I still find the English dictionary the most interesting book in the English language.

ALBERT JAY NOCK

Just the knowledge that a good book is awaiting one at the end of a long day makes that day happier.

KATHLEEN NORRIS

I love the solitude of reading. I love the deep dive into someone else's story, the delicious ache of a last page. I love the wide basket in which shining fruits rest together on a table. The sense of gathering, the gleam, seems similar to the bounty offered by an anthology.

Reading is, simply, the best thing I ever do in my life. My son and I curl up together each evening, hungry for "our book," our story, our private world. He goes nowhere without a satchel of books. He can "amuse himself" anywhere. We pass it on. As he falls asleep, I retreat back to my bedside table with its precarious skyscraper of reading matter, treasures waiting to be held.

NAOMI SHIHAB NYE

A story with a moral appended is like the bite of a mosquito. It bores you, and then injects a stinging drop to irritate your conscience.

O. HENRY

I think that reading a novel is almost next best to having something to do.

MARGARET OLIPHANT

Great books endure because they help us interpret our lives. It's a personal quest, this grappling with the world and ourselves, and we need all the help we can get. The fact that there are people who came before us and wrote so much down in books is consoling. We stand on their shoulders.

MICHAEL OLMERT

Don't read science fiction books. It'll look bad if you die in bed with one on the nightstand. Always read stuff that will make you look good if you die in the middle of it.

P. J. O'ROURKE

There's a paradox in rereading. You read the first time for rediscovery: an encounter with the confirming emotions. But you reread for discovery: you go to the known to figure out the workings of the unknown, the why of the familiar how.

CYNTHIA OZICK

You cannot embark on life, that on-off coach ride, once again when it is over, but if you have a book in your hand, no matter how complex or difficult to understand that book may be, when you have finished it, you can, if you wish, go back to the beginning, read it again, and thus understand that which is difficult and, with it, understand life as well.

ORHAN PAMUK

This is not a novel to be tossed aside lightly. It should be thrown with great force.

DOROTHY PARKER, in a book review

A philosopher at a liberal arts college once remarked to me that "I used to believe that John Updike had nothing to say, and then I thought, 'Then why have I been reading him for thirty years?'"

KYLE A. PASEWARK

Books, like good friends, should be few and well chosen.

SAMUEL PATERSON*
*The quotation is often attributed to Bronson Alcott and Louisa May Alcott

Nevertheless, Sir, there are some things more fit to be looked at than others. For instance, there is nothing more fit to be looked at than the outside of a book . . . It is, as I may say from repeated experience, a pure and unmixed pleasure to have a goodly volume lying before you, and to know you need not open it unless you please.

THOMAS L. PEACOCK

You make an acquaintance with a book as you do with a person. After ten or fifteen pages, you know with whom you have to deal. When you have a good book, you really have something of importance. Books are as important as friends and maybe more so.

SHIMON PERES

For readers, there must be a million autobiographies.

STAN PERSKY

Literature and vocabulary don't go together. Otherwise, a dictionary would be the greatest literary masterpiece.

LAWRENCE J. PETERS

Books come at my call and return when I desire them. They are never out of humor and they answer all my questions with readiness.

PETRARCH

Kitchen and pantry cabinets can be commandeered in the fight to find bookshelf space, and a family's eating habits can be changed. When china is displaced by paper plates, there is no longer any reason why books cannot be stored in the dishwasher too. An empty refrigerator is an excellent repository for the most valuable of books because books like low temperatures best.

HENRY PETROSKI

I divide all readers into two classes: those who read to remember and those who read to forget.

WILLIAM LYON PHELPS

It is the books we read before middle life that do most to mold our characters and influence our lives.

ROBERT PITMAN

He [Pliny the Elder] used to say that "no book was so bad but some good might be got out of it."

PLINY THE YOUNGER

In reading some books, we occupy ourselves chiefly with the thoughts of the author; in perusing others, chiefly with our own.

EDGAR ALLAN POE

When something can be read without effort, great effort has gone into its writing.

ENRIQUE JARDIEL PONCELA

[The library] is like a place of sacredness. If we were fools at one time, perhaps we will not be fools tomorrow, if we study.

TOM PORTER

Some books are to be read in an hour, and returned to the shelf. Others require a lifetime to savor their richness.

LAWRENCE C. POWELL

Man is the animal who weeps and laughs, and writes. If the first Prometheus brought fire from heaven in a fennel-stalk, the last will take it back in a book.

JOHN COWPER POWYS

Few children learn to read books by themselves. Someone has to lure them into the wonderful world of the written word. Someone has to show them the way.

ORVILLE PRESCOTT

THE GOLDFISH

The gaping goldfish in his bowl
   I'm sure is happy, on the whole;
He has that silly, vacant look
   Because he's never read a book.

A. G. Prys-Jones

In books I have traveled, not only to other worlds, but into my own. I learned who I was and who I wanted to be, what I might aspire to, and what I might dare to dream about my world and myself.

I read *A Wrinkle in Time* three times in a row once, when I was twelve, because I couldn't bear for it to end.

I would be most content if my children grew up to be the kind of people who think decorating consists mostly of building enough bookcases.

Of all the many things in which we recognize some universal comfort—God, sex, food, family, friends—reading seems to be the one in which the comfort is most undersung, at least publicly, although it was really all I thought of, or felt, when I was eating up book after book, running away from home while sitting in (a) chair, traveling around the world and yet never leaving the room. I did not read from a sense of superiority, or advancement, or even learning. I read because I loved it more than any other activity on earth.

Anna Quindlen

Restaurant reading is not what it used to be. We can't kill half a day dominating a booth and drinking coffee or whatever else. We actually have to eat something . . . How do we place our book in an accessible location on the table and make it stay open while wielding our cutlery? That's the real problem.

Tom Raabe

When writers refer to themselves as "we" and to the reader as "you," it's two against one.

JUDITH RASCOE

Emerson and Thoreau are the people that I read when I'm feeling bad. I come away from reading them feeling better about myself, and the world, and my friends, and the country.

ROBERT D. RICHARDSON, JR.

Reading was not one of my boyhood passions. Girls, or rather the absence of girls, drove me to it.

MORDECAI RICHLER

Friends: people who borrow my books and set wet glasses on them.

EDWIN ARLINGTON ROBINSON

Some men borrow books; some men steal books, and others beg presentation copies from the author.

JAMES ROCHE

Reading makes immigrants of us all. It takes us away from home, but, most important, it finds homes for us everywhere.

HAZEL ROCHMAN

A breakfast without a newspaper is a horse without a saddle. You are just riding bareback. Take away my ham, take away my eggs, even my chili, but leave my newspaper.

There ain't nothing that breaks up homes, country, and nations like somebody publishing their memoirs.

People only learn through two things. One is reading and the other is association with smarter people.

WILL ROGERS

Normally, the books which do good and the books which healthy people find interesting are those which are not in the least of the sugar-candy variety, but which, while portraying foulness and suffering when they must be portrayed, yet have a joyous as well as a noble side.

THEODORE ROOSEVELT

There may be no more pleasing picture in this world than that of a child peering into a book—the past and the future entrancing each other.

ROGER ROSENBLATT

The book is the vessel that contains all the ideas that are good and important in our culture. As such, it must be cherished, preserved, and protected.

ANDREW ROSS

Literature takes a habit of mind that has disappeared. It requires silence, some form of isolation, and sustained concentration in the presence of an enigmatic thing.

PHILIP ROTH

Children's books aren't textbooks. Their primary purpose isn't supposed to be "Pick this up and it will teach you this." It's not how literature should be. You probably do learn something from every book you pick up, but it might be simply how to laugh. It doesn't have to be a slap-you-in-the-face moral every time.

J. K. ROWLING

Life being short and the quiet hours of it few, we ought to waste none of them in reading valueless books.

All books are divisible into two classes: the books of the hour and the books of all time.

What do we, as a nation, care about books? How much do you

think we spend altogether on our libraries, public or private, as compared with what we spend on our horses?

JOHN RUSKIN

There's nothing to match curling up with a good book when there's a repair job to be done around the house.

JOE RYAN

I have always cherished valueless books; that is, books whose chief worth is their simple readability. Page-turners, they are sometimes disparagingly called, as if providing the reader with a reason to turn the page were contemptible, let alone easy.

WITOLD RYBCZYNSKI

By elevating your reading, you improve your writing or at least tickle your thinking.

WILLIAM SAFIRE

One of the greatest gifts adults can give—to their offspring and to their society—is to read to children.

CARL SAGAN

There are books in which the footnotes, or the comments scrawled by some reader's hand in the margin, are more interesting than the text. The world is one of these books.

GEORGE SANTAYANA

It was in books I encountered the universe—assimilated, classified, labeled, pondered, still formidable.

JEAN-PAUL SARTRE

Books . . . are like lobster shells. We surround ourselves with 'em, then we grow out of 'em and leave 'em behind, as evidence of our earlier stages of development.

DOROTHY SAYERS

Only those writers profit us whose understanding is quicker, more lucid than our own, by whose brain we indeed think for a time, who quicken our thoughts, and lead us whither alone we could not find our way.

ARTHUR SCHOPENHAUER

Nurse to man on a hospital gurney: "They're going to take you back to surgery, professor. Dr. Bickel got confused and removed your glossary instead of your appendix."

HARLEY SCHWADRON — cartoon caption

The big advantage of a book is that it's very easy to rewind. Close it and you're right back at the beginning.

Sunday paper is the worst. Weekend. You want to relax. "Oh, by the way, here's a thousand pages of information you had no idea about." How can they tell you everything they know every single day of the week and then have this much left over on Sunday when nothing's going on?

A bookstore is one of the only pieces of physical evidence we have that people are still thinking. And I like the way it breaks down into fiction and nonfiction. In other words, these people are lying, and these people are telling the truth. That's the way the world should be.

JERRY SEINFELD

Now this is what I call workmanship. There is nothing on earth more exquisite than a bonny book, with well-placed columns of rich black writing in beautiful borders, and illuminated pictures cunningly inset. But nowadays, instead of looking at books, people read them.

GEORGE BERNARD SHAW

Read Homer once, and you can read no more,
For all books else appear so mean, so poor,

Verse will seem prose; but still persist to read,
And Homer will be all the books you need.

> JOHN SHEFFIELD,
> DUKE OF BUCKINGHAMSHIRE

Books are the opposite of television. They are slow, engaging, inspiring, intellect-arousing, and creativity-spurring.

> DAVID SHENK, author of *Data Smog:*
> *Surviving the Information Glut*

The right book at the right time may mean more in a person's life than anything else.

> LEE SHIPPEY

My personal hobbies are reading, listening to music, and silence.

> EDITH SITWELL

In truth, the reader should be as carefully and patiently trained as the writer.

> OSBERT SITWELL

On the whole, perhaps, it is the great readers rather than the great writers who are entirely to be envied. They pluck the fruits, and are spared the trouble of rearing them.

> ALEXANDER SMITH

What I like in a good author is not what he says, but what he whispers.

The world, as I know from my books, is full of abominable evil; even some of these books have never been returned.

> LOGAN PEARSALL SMITH

We should accustom the mind to keep the best company by reading only the best books.

> SYDNEY SMITH

Books extend our narrow present back into a limitless past. They show us the mistakes of the men before us and share with us recipes for human success. There's nothing to be done which books will not help us do better.

T. V. SMITH

Employ your time in improving yourself by other men's writing so that you shall come easily by what others have labored hard for.

SOCRATES

Writers, of course, are readers as well. When I taught creative writing I didn't produce writers, I was really teaching reading.

SUSAN SONTAG

Books are a hindrance to persisting stupidity.

SPANISH PROVERB

The man who never reads will never be read; he who never quotes will never be quoted. He who will not use the thoughts of other men's brains proves he has no brain of his own.

CHARLES H. SPURGEON

Reading is to the mind what exercise is to the body.

RICHARD STEELE

Hard-covered books break up friendships. You lend a hard-covered book to a friend and when he doesn't return it, you get mad at him. It makes you mean and petty. But 25-cent books are different.

JOHN STEINBECK

As library annual reports have indicated for some time—here one need only cite, for example, the famous passage found in column 1,303 of the *Annual Report of the Library at Alexandria* for 250 B.C.—the disappearance, exchange, and loss of umbrellas is a phenomenon closely associated with libraries.

NORMAN STEVENS

Biography . . . performs for us some of the work of fiction, reminding us, that is, of the truly mangled tissue of man's nature and how huge faults and virtues cohabit and persevere in the same character.

ROBERT LOUIS STEVENSON

Why pay a dollar for a bookmark? Why not use the dollar for a bookmark?

FRED STOLLER

It's not macho to read a book? Nonsense. Reading is a stouthearted activity, disporting courage, keenness, stick-to-it-ness. It is also, in my experience, one of the most thrilling and enduring delights of life, equal to a home run, a slam-dunk, or breaking the four-minute mile.

IRVING STONE

My theory is that people who don't like mystery stories are anarchists.

REX STOUT

A great book should leave you with many experiences, and slightly exhausted at the end. You live several lives while reading it.

WILLIAM STYRON

E-books *are* getting better and better, but new technologies don't triumph just because they work well; they have to solve a real problem. And for most people the physical book offers no problems at all. The book—portable, intuitive to use—is an almost perfect technology.

JAMES SUROWIECKI

I'll spend the rest of my life reading, and because I'd rather read than do anything else, I don't look forward to years of hopeless, black despair. Most men who are in for life are filled with bitterness and hatred for the unkind fate that led them to such a horrible end.

WILLIE SUTTON, convicted bank robber

Books, the children of the brain.

When I am reading a book, whether wise or silly, it seems to me to be alive and talking to me.

JONATHAN SWIFT

Reading sweeps the cobwebs away; it increases our power of concentration; it makes us more interesting to be around, and it strengthens our ability to glean truth from God's Word.

CHARLES R. SWINDOLL

Books contain the power to lift us from the milieu in which we live and work. It is as though they have the capacity of transporting us to another realm of being.

LUCI SWINDOLL

Public schools ceased to emphasize the development of reading skills starting in the '60s, around the same time that TV became ubiquitous. For this reason, most Americans born after 1970 are image-oriented: They spend more time looking at pictures than at the printed word. This is a development of fearful significance, since a culture based solely on images is condemned to shallowness. If you doubt this, consider the effect of TV on politics.

TERRY TEACHOUT

A candidate for success should always carry a library. You can make the minutes count, whether waiting at the airport to board an airplane or holding a strap on the subway. You may be catching up on office work, or analyzing current events, or simply reading to improve your mind and widen your knowledge . . . By having books and papers with you at all times—your portable library—you can always accomplish something that will advance your career that much more quickly.

JOHN M. TEMPLETON

What is a diary as a rule? A document useful to the person who keeps it. Dull to the contemporary who reads it. Invaluable to the student, centuries afterward, who treasures it.

HELEN TERRY

My education was the liberty I had to read indiscriminately and all the time with my eyes hanging out.

DYLAN THOMAS

Books must be read as deliberately and reservedly as they are written.

Books are the treasured wealth of the world and the fit inheritance of generations and nations.

How many a man has dated a new era in his life from the reading of a book. The book exists for us perchance which will explain our miracles and reveal new ones.

HENRY DAVID THOREAU

We all have our literary idiosyncracies and blind spots. H. L. Mencken used to pray to God for guidance, so that he might be made to see what merit there was in the works of D. H. Lawrence.

One great advantage which poetry has over prose—one sense in which, we might even say, it is considerably more beautiful—is that it fills up space approximately three times as fast.

Fables, of course, are the oldest form of literary expression. You know Aesop. Nobody knows exactly when he lived, but Webster put it at 580 B.C. That is to say, more than twenty-five centuries ago. After all those 2,500 years, two expressions of his are commonly used today. We don't go a week without using one or the other: "the lion's share" and "sour grapes."

JAMES THURBER

There is hardly a pioneer's hut which does not contain a few odd volumes of Shakespeare. I remember reading the feudal drama of *Henry V* for the first time, in a log cabin.

ALEXIS DE TOCQUEVILLE
commenting on the reading habits of Americans in his 1840 book *Democracy in America*, vol. 2

Fantasy is escapist, and that is its glory. If a soldier is imprisoned by the enemy, don't we consider it his duty to escape? The moneylenders, the know-nothings, the authoritarians have us all in prison. If we value the freedom of mind and soul, if we're partisans of liberty, then it's our plain duty to escape, and to take as many people with us as we can!

J. R. R. TOLKIEN

Instead of going to Paris to attend lectures, go to the public library, and you won't come out for twenty years, if you really wish to learn.

LEO TOLSTOY

I read because my father read to me. And because he'd read to me, when my time came I knew intuitively there is a torch that is supposed to be passed from one generation to the next. And through countless nights of reading I began to realize that when enough of the torchbearers—parents and teachers—stop passing the torches, a culture begins to die.

Reading is the single most important factor in America today . . . The more you read, the more you know. The more you know, the smarter you grow. The smarter you are, the longer you stay in school and the more diplomas you earn. The more diplomas you have, the more days you are employed. The more diplomas you have, the more your children will achieve in school. And the more diplomas you have, the longer you will live.

JIM TRELEASE

Education . . . has produced a vast population able to read but unable to distinguish what is worth reading.

G. M. TREVELYAN

The habit of reading is the only one I know in which there is no alloy. It lasts when all other pleasures fade. It will be there to support you when all other resources are gone . . . It will make your hours pleasant to you as long as you live.

ANTHONY TROLLOPE

The worst thing in the world is when records are destroyed. The destruction of the Alexandrian Library and also the destruction of the great libraries in Rome. Those were terrible things, and one was done by the Moslems and the others by the Christians, but there's no difference between them when they're working for propaganda purposes.

HARRY S. TRUMAN

To a historian, libraries are food, shelter, and even muse.

Without books, history is silent, literature dumb, science crippled, thought and speculation at a standstill. They are engines of change, windows on the world, lighthouses erected in the sea of time.

BARBARA TUCHMAN

Alexander Tvarovsky, editor-in-chief of the Russian literary magazine *Novy Mir*, took some manuscripts home to read in bed one evening in 1962. He skimmed through them quickly, tossing most of them into a pile of rejects. He came to a manuscript by one Aleksandr Solzhenitsyn, a writer he did not know, who had titled it simply *One Day in the Life of Ivan Denisovich*. After reading the first ten lines, he told a friend later, "suddenly I felt that I couldn't read it like this. I had to do something appropriate to the occasion. So I got up. I put on my best black suit, a white shirt with a starched collar, a tie, and my good shoes. Then I sat at my desk and read a new classic."

ALEXANDER TVAROVSKY

Be careful about reading health books. You might die of a misprint.

The man who does not read good books has no advantage over the man who *can't* read them.

Asked whether he liked books, Mark Twain said that he liked a thin book because it would steady a table, a leather volume because it would strop a razor, and a heavy book because it could be thrown at a cat.

MARK TWAIN

I was born with the impression that what happened in books was much more reasonable, and interesting, and real, in some ways, than what happened in life.

ANNE TYLER

By bedside and easy chair, books promise a cozy, swift and silent release from this world into another, with no current involved but the free and scarcely detectable crackle of brain cells. For ease of access and speed of storage, books are tough to beat.

One's collection comes to symbolize the content of one's mind. Books read in childhood, in yearning adolescence, at college and in the first self-conscious years of adulthood travel along, often, with readers as they move from house to house. My mother's college texts, I remember, sat untouched in a corner of our country bookcase, radiating the satisfactions of Renaissance poetry and Greek drama while being slowly hollowed by silverfish.

JOHN UPDIKE

A classic is a book that doesn't have to be written again.

CARL VAN DOREN

Some books are fast and some are slow, but no book can be understood if it is taken at the wrong speed.

MARK VAN DOREN

Books rule the world, at least those nations which have a written language.

VOLTAIRE

Any reviewer who expresses rage and loathing for a novel is preposterous. He or she is like a person who has put on a full armor and attacked a hot fudge sundae.

I once said at a birthday party that I had of course plagiarized all my material, that nobody'd been able to catch me, and that now I'd finally reveal where I'd gotten this stuff—I said I got it from *The Theory of the Leisure Class*. Somebody at the party later went home to Philadelphia and discovered at the public library that it hadn't been checked out in twelve years.

KURT VONNEGUT, JR.

Ultimately, both reader and writer have the same goal . . . The writer wants ideas to glide smoothly from the mind to the page, and the reader wants ideas to glide smoothly from the page to the mind. The only plausible means to satisfy both seems to be an agreement upon the idea's mode of travel: a shared system that becomes so familiar to both writer and reader as to be second nature.

MARILYN VOS SAVANT

To be able to see in one's mind another's journey or achievement, another's rationale of the solution to a problem is as close as one can get to actual experience. Books do that. They open our minds to wondering and thinking about why we are here, to trying to do the best we can, and to the realization that anything less on our part is to throw away a large portion of the time each of us has been allotted on this earth.

G. KINGSLEY WARD

Man builds no structure which outlives a book.

EUGENE WARE ("Ironquill")

I always turn first to the sports pages, which record people's accomplishments. The front page has nothing but man's failures.

EARL WARREN

I conceive that a knowledge of books is the basis on which all other knowledge rests.

GEORGE WASHINGTON

He had read Shakespeare and found him weak in chemistry.

H. G. WELLS

It had been startling and disappointing to me to find out that story books had been written by *people*, that books were not natural wonders, coming up of themselves like grass.

I live in gratitude to my parents for initiating me—and as early as I begged for it, without keeping me waiting—into knowledge of the word, into reading and spelling, by way of the alphabet. They taught it to me at home in time for me to begin to read before starting to school. I believe the alphabet is no longer considered an essential piece of equipment for traveling through life. In my day it was the keystone to knowledge. You learned the alphabet as you learned to count to ten, as you learned "Now I lay me" and the Lord's Prayer and your father's and mother's name and address and telephone number, all in case you were lost.

EUDORA WELTY

Reading is the work of the alert mind, is demanding, and under ideal conditions produces finally a sort of ecstasy. This gives the experience of reading a sublimity and power unequaled by any other form of communication.

E. B. WHITE

Books are to be called for and supplied on the assumption that the process of reading is not a half-sleep; but in the highest sense an exercise, a gymnasium struggle; that the reader is to do something for himself.

WALT WHITMAN

The greatest fun in reading aloud lies in the adventure of the thing—the sense of taking a child on an exploration of a fascinating territory into which you alone have penetrated.

LEONARD WIBBERLEY

If one cannot enjoy reading a book over and over again, there is no use in reading it at all.

To tell people what to read is as a rule either useless or harmful, for the true appreciation of literature is a question of temperament, not of teaching . . . But to tell people what not to read is a very different matter, and I venture to recommend it as a mission to the University Extension Scheme.

OSCAR WILDE

The best thing about celebrity is that it gets your books read.

GEORGE WILL

Books were my pass to personal freedom. I learned to read at age three, and soon discovered there was a whole world to conquer that went beyond our farm in Mississippi.

OPRAH WINFREY

The final goal of reading is not merely to derive information from a text efficiently but to be able to evaluate that information—in other words, to read critically. Writings speak for their authors, and like other humans, authors can be prejudiced, ignorant of important facts and concepts, and mendacious—or wise, honest, knowledgeable, and reliable. A critical reader thinks carefully about what he or she reads, evaluates it, tests its logic and its facts, seeks its strengths and weaknesses. Critical readers learn more and certainly enjoy their reading more than passive readers.

W. ROSS WINTEROWD

Fiction is like a spider's web, attached ever so lightly perhaps, but still attached to life at all four corners.

To write down one's impressions of *Hamlet* as one reads it year after year would be virtually to record one's own autobiography, for as we know more of life, so Shakespeare comments on what we know.

I have sometimes dreamt that when the Day of Judgment dawns and the great conquerors and lawyers and statesmen come to receive their rewards—their crowns, their laurels, their names carved indelibly upon imperishable marble—the Almighty will turn to Peter and will say, not without a certain envy when He sees us coming with our books under our arms, "Look, these need no reward. We have nothing to give them here. They have loved reading."

VIRGINIA WOOLF

Dreams, books, are each a world, and books, we know,
Are a substantial world, both pure and good.
Round these, with tendrils strong as flesh and blood,
Our pastime and our happiness will grow.

WILLIAM WORDSWORTH

What's another word for *Thesaurus*?

STEVEN WRIGHT

Across time and generations, books carry the thoughts and feelings, the essence, of the human spirit.

PHILIP YANCEY

To me the charm of an encyclopedia is that it knows, and I needn't.

FRANCIS YEATS-BROWN

I think it is good that books *still* exist, but they make me sleepy.

FRANK ZAPPA

POETRY

101 GREAT AMERICAN POEMS, Edited by The American Poetry & Literacy Project. (0-486-40158-8)

100 BEST-LOVED POEMS, Edited by Philip Smith. (0-486-28553-7)

ENGLISH ROMANTIC POETRY: An Anthology, Edited by Stanley Appelbaum. (0-486-29282-7)

THE INFERNO, Dante Alighieri. Translated and with notes by Henry Wadsworth Longfellow. (0-486-44288-8)

PARADISE LOST, John Milton. Introduction and Notes by John A. Himes. (0-486-44287-X)

SPOON RIVER ANTHOLOGY, Edgar Lee Masters. (0-486-27275-3)

SELECTED CANTERBURY TALES, Geoffrey Chaucer. (0-486-28241-4)

SELECTED POEMS, Emily Dickinson. (0-486-26466-1)

LEAVES OF GRASS: The Original 1855 Edition, Walt Whitman. (0-486-45676-5)

COMPLETE SONNETS, William Shakespeare. (0-486-26686-9)

THE RAVEN AND OTHER FAVORITE POEMS, Edgar Allan Poe. (0-486-26685-0)

ENGLISH VICTORIAN POETRY: An Anthology, Edited by Paul Negri. (0-486-40425-0)

SELECTED POEMS, Walt Whitman. (0-486-26878-0)

THE ROAD NOT TAKEN AND OTHER POEMS, Robert Frost. (0-486-27550-7)

AFRICAN-AMERICAN POETRY: An Anthology, 1773-1927, Edited by Joan R. Sherman. (0-486-29604-0)

GREAT SHORT POEMS, Edited by Paul Negri. (0-486-41105-2)

THE RIME OF THE ANCIENT MARINER, Samuel Taylor Coleridge. (0-486-27266-4)

THE WASTE LAND, PRUFROCK AND OTHER POEMS, T. S. Eliot. (0-486-40061-1)

SONG OF MYSELF, Walt Whitman. (0-486-41410-8)

AENEID, Vergil. (0-486-28749-1)

SONGS FOR THE OPEN ROAD: Poems of Travel and Adventure, Edited by The American Poetry & Literacy Project. (0-486-40646-6)

SONGS OF INNOCENCE AND SONGS OF EXPERIENCE, William Blake. (0-486-27051-3)

WORLD WAR ONE BRITISH POETS: Brooke, Owen, Sassoon, Rosenberg and Others, Edited by Candace Ward. (0-486-29568-0)

GREAT SONNETS, Edited by Paul Negri. (0-486-28052-7)

CHRISTMAS CAROLS: Complete Verses, Edited by Shane Weller. (0-486-27397-0)

DOVER THRIFT EDITIONS

POETRY

GREAT POEMS BY AMERICAN WOMEN: An Anthology, Edited by Susan L. Rattiner. (0-486-40164-2)

FAVORITE POEMS, Henry Wadsworth Longfellow. (0-486-27273-7)

BHAGAVADGITA, Translated by Sir Edwin Arnold. (0-486-27782-8)

ESSAY ON MAN AND OTHER POEMS, Alexander Pope. (0-486-28053-5)

GREAT LOVE POEMS, Edited by Shane Weller. (0-486-27284-2)

DOVER BEACH AND OTHER POEMS, Matthew Arnold. (0-486-28037-3)

THE SHOOTING OF DAN MCGREW AND OTHER POEMS, Robert Service. (0-486-27556-6)

THE BALLAD OF READING GAOL AND OTHER POEMS, Oscar Wilde. (0-486-27072-6)

SELECTED POEMS OF RUMI, Jalalu'l-Din Rumi. (0-486-41583-X)

SELECTED POEMS OF GERARD MANLEY HOPKINS, Gerard Manley Hopkins. Edited and with an Introduction by Bob Blaisdell. (0-486-47867-X)

RENASCENCE AND OTHER POEMS, Edna St. Vincent Millay. (0-486-26873-X)

THE RUBÁIYÁT OF OMAR KHAYYÁM: First and Fifth Editions, Edward FitzGerald. (0-486-26467-X)

TO MY HUSBAND AND OTHER POEMS, Anne Bradstreet. (0-486-41408-6)

LITTLE ORPHANT ANNIE AND OTHER POEMS, James Whitcomb Riley. (0-486-28260-0)

IMAGIST POETRY: AN ANTHOLOGY, Edited by Bob Blaisdell. (0-486-40875-2)

FIRST FIG AND OTHER POEMS, Edna St. Vincent Millay. (0-486-41104-4)

GREAT SHORT POEMS FROM ANTIQUITY TO THE TWENTIETH CENTURY, Edited by Dorothy Belle Pollack. (0-486-47876-9)

THE FLOWERS OF EVIL & PARIS SPLEEN: Selected Poems, Charles Baudelaire. Translated by Wallace Fowlie. (0-486-47545-X)

CIVIL WAR SHORT STORIES AND POEMS, Edited by Bob Blaisdell. (0-486-48226-X)

EARLY POEMS, Edna St. Vincent Millay. (0-486-43672-1)

JABBERWOCKY AND OTHER POEMS, Lewis Carroll. (0-486-41582-1)

THE METAMORPHOSES: Selected Stories in Verse, Ovid. (0-486-42758-7)

IDYLLS OF THE KING, Alfred, Lord Tennyson. Edited by W. J. Rolfe. (0-486-43795-7)

A BOY'S WILL AND NORTH OF BOSTON, Robert Frost. (0-486-26866-7)

100 FAVORITE ENGLISH AND IRISH POEMS, Edited by Clarence C. Strowbridge. (0-486-44429-5)

FICTION

FLATLAND: A ROMANCE OF MANY DIMENSIONS, Edwin A. Abbott.
(0-486-27263-X)

PRIDE AND PREJUDICE, Jane Austen. (0-486-28473-5)

CIVIL WAR SHORT STORIES AND POEMS, Edited by Bob Blaisdell.
(0-486-48226-X)

THE DECAMERON: Selected Tales, Giovanni Boccaccio. Edited by Bob Blaisdell. (0-486-41113-3)

JANE EYRE, Charlotte Brontë. (0-486-42449-9)

WUTHERING HEIGHTS, Emily Brontë. (0-486-29256-8)

THE THIRTY-NINE STEPS, John Buchan. (0-486-28201-5)

ALICE'S ADVENTURES IN WONDERLAND, Lewis Carroll. (0-486-27543-4)

MY ÁNTONIA, Willa Cather. (0-486-28240-6)

THE AWAKENING, Kate Chopin. (0-486-27786-0)

HEART OF DARKNESS, Joseph Conrad. (0-486-26464-5)

LORD JIM, Joseph Conrad. (0-486-40650-4)

THE RED BADGE OF COURAGE, Stephen Crane. (0-486-26465-3)

THE WORLD'S GREATEST SHORT STORIES, Edited by James Daley.
(0-486-44716-2)

A CHRISTMAS CAROL, Charles Dickens. (0-486-26865-9)

GREAT EXPECTATIONS, Charles Dickens. (0-486-41586-4)

A TALE OF TWO CITIES, Charles Dickens. (0-486-40651-2)

CRIME AND PUNISHMENT, Fyodor Dostoyevsky. Translated by Constance Garnett. (0-486-41587-2)

THE ADVENTURES OF SHERLOCK HOLMES, Sir Arthur Conan Doyle.
(0-486-47491-7)

THE HOUND OF THE BASKERVILLES, Sir Arthur Conan Doyle. (0-486-28214-7)

BLAKE: PROPHET AGAINST EMPIRE, David V. Erdman. (0-486-26719-9)

WHERE ANGELS FEAR TO TREAD, E. M. Forster. (0-486-27791-7)

BEOWULF, Translated by R. K. Gordon. (0-486-27264-8)

THE RETURN OF THE NATIVE, Thomas Hardy. (0-486-43165-7)

THE SCARLET LETTER, Nathaniel Hawthorne. (0-486-28048-9)

SIDDHARTHA, Hermann Hesse. (0-486-40653-9)

THE ODYSSEY, Homer. (0-486-40654-7)

THE TURN OF THE SCREW, Henry James. (0-486-26684-2)

DUBLINERS, James Joyce. (0-486-26870-5)

FICTION

THE METAMORPHOSIS AND OTHER STORIES, Franz Kafka. (0-486-29030-1)

SONS AND LOVERS, D. H. Lawrence. (0-486-42121-X)

THE CALL OF THE WILD, Jack London. (0-486-26472-6)

GREAT AMERICAN SHORT STORIES, Edited by Paul Negri. (0-486-42119-8)

THE GOLD-BUG AND OTHER TALES, Edgar Allan Poe. (0-486-26875-6)

ANTHEM, Ayn Rand. (0-486-49277-X)

FRANKENSTEIN, Mary Shelley. (0-486-28211-2)

THE JUNGLE, Upton Sinclair. (0-486-41923-1)

THREE LIVES, Gertrude Stein. (0-486-28059-4)

THE STRANGE CASE OF DR. JEKYLL AND MR. HYDE, Robert Louis Stevenson. (0-486-26688-5)

DRACULA, Bram Stoker. (0-486-41109-5)

UNCLE TOM'S CABIN, Harriet Beecher Stowe. (0-486-44028-1)

ADVENTURES OF HUCKLEBERRY FINN, Mark Twain. (0-486-28061-6)

THE ADVENTURES OF TOM SAWYER, Mark Twain. (0-486-40077-8)

CANDIDE, Voltaire. Edited by Francois-Marie Arouet. (0-486-26689-3)

THE COUNTRY OF THE BLIND: and Other Science-Fiction Stories, H. G. Wells. Edited by Martin Gardner. (0-486-48289-8)

THE WAR OF THE WORLDS, H. G. Wells. (0-486-29506-0)

ETHAN FROME, Edith Wharton. (0-486-26690-7)

THE PICTURE OF DORIAN GRAY, Oscar Wilde. (0-486-27807-7)

MONDAY OR TUESDAY: Eight Stories, Virginia Woolf. (0-486-29453-6)

NONFICTION

POETICS, Aristotle. (0-486-29577-X)

MEDITATIONS, Marcus Aurelius. (0-486-29823-X)

THE WAY OF PERFECTION, St. Teresa of Avila. Edited and Translated by
E. Allison Peers. (0-486-48451-3)

THE DEVIL'S DICTIONARY, Ambrose Bierce. (0-486-27542-6)

GREAT SPEECHES OF THE 20TH CENTURY, Edited by Bob Blaisdell.
(0-486-47467-4)

THE COMMUNIST MANIFESTO AND OTHER REVOLUTIONARY WRITINGS:
Marx, Marat, Paine, Mao Tse-Tung, Gandhi and Others, Edited by Bob Blaisdell.
(0-486-42465-0)

INFAMOUS SPEECHES: From Robespierre to Osama bin Laden, Edited by Bob
Blaisdell. (0-486-47849-1)

GREAT ENGLISH ESSAYS: From Bacon to Chesterton, Edited by Bob Blaisdell.
(0-486-44082-6)

GREEK AND ROMAN ORATORY, Edited by Bob Blaisdell. (0-486-49622-8)

THE UNITED STATES CONSTITUTION: The Full Text with Supplementary
Materials, Edited and with supplementary materials by Bob Blaisdell.
(0-486-47166-7)

GREAT SPEECHES BY NATIVE AMERICANS, Edited by Bob Blaisdell.
(0-486-41122-2)

GREAT SPEECHES BY AFRICAN AMERICANS: Frederick Douglass, Sojourner
Truth, Dr. Martin Luther King, Jr., Barack Obama, and Others, Edited by
James Daley. (0-486-44761-8)

GREAT SPEECHES BY AMERICAN WOMEN, Edited by James Daley.
(0-486-46141-6)

HISTORY'S GREATEST SPEECHES, Edited by James Daley. (0-486-49739-9)

GREAT INAUGURAL ADDRESSES, Edited by James Daley. (0-486-44577-1)

GREAT SPEECHES ON GAY RIGHTS, Edited by James Daley. (0-486-47512-3)

ON THE ORIGIN OF SPECIES: By Means of Natural Selection, Charles Darwin.
(0-486-45006-6)

NARRATIVE OF THE LIFE OF FREDERICK DOUGLASS, Frederick Douglass.
(0-486-28499-9)

THE SOULS OF BLACK FOLK, W. E. B. Du Bois. (0-486-28041-1)

NATURE AND OTHER ESSAYS, Ralph Waldo Emerson. (0-486-46947-6)

SELF-RELIANCE AND OTHER ESSAYS, Ralph Waldo Emerson. (0-486-27790-9)

THE LIFE OF OLAUDAH EQUIANO, Olaudah Equiano. (0-486-40661-X)

WIT AND WISDOM FROM POOR RICHARD'S ALMANACK, Benjamin Franklin.
(0-486-40891-4)

THE AUTOBIOGRAPHY OF BENJAMIN FRANKLIN, Benjamin Franklin.
(0-486-29073-5)

NONFICTION

THE DECLARATION OF INDEPENDENCE AND OTHER GREAT DOCUMENTS OF AMERICAN HISTORY: 1775-1865, Edited by John Grafton. (0-486-41124-9)

INCIDENTS IN THE LIFE OF A SLAVE GIRL, Harriet Jacobs. (0-486-41931-2)

GREAT SPEECHES, Abraham Lincoln. (0-486-26872-1)

THE WIT AND WISDOM OF ABRAHAM LINCOLN: A Book of Quotations, Abraham Lincoln. Edited by Bob Blaisdell. (0-486-44097-4)

THE SECOND TREATISE OF GOVERNMENT AND A LETTER CONCERNING TOLERATION, John Locke. (0-486-42464-2)

THE PRINCE, Niccolò Machiavelli. (0-486-27274-5)

MICHEL DE MONTAIGNE: Selected Essays, Michel de Montaigne. Translated by Charles Cotton. Edited by William Carew Hazlitt. (0-486-48603-6)

UTOPIA, Sir Thomas More. (0-486-29583-4)

BEYOND GOOD AND EVIL: Prelude to a Philosophy of the Future, Friedrich Nietzsche. (0-486-29868-X)

TWELVE YEARS A SLAVE, Solomon Northup. (0-486-78962-4)

COMMON SENSE, Thomas Paine. (0-486-29602-4)

BOOK OF AFRICAN-AMERICAN QUOTATIONS, Edited by Joslyn Pine. (0-486-47589-1)

THE TRIAL AND DEATH OF SOCRATES: Four Dialogues, Plato. (0-486-27066-1)

THE REPUBLIC, Plato. (0-486-41121-4)

SIX GREAT DIALOGUES: Apology, Crito, Phaedo, Phaedrus, Symposium, The Republic, Plato. Translated by Benjamin Jowett. (0-486-45465-7)

WOMEN'S WIT AND WISDOM: A Book of Quotations, Edited by Susan L. Rattiner. (0-486-41123-0)

GREAT SPEECHES, Franklin Delano Roosevelt. (0-486-40894-9)

THE CONFESSIONS OF ST. AUGUSTINE, St. Augustine. (0-486-42466-9)

A MODEST PROPOSAL AND OTHER SATIRICAL WORKS, Jonathan Swift. (0-486-28759-9)

THE IMITATION OF CHRIST, Thomas à Kempis. Translated by Aloysius Croft and Harold Bolton. (0-486-43185-1)

CIVIL DISOBEDIENCE AND OTHER ESSAYS, Henry David Thoreau. (0-486-27563-9)

WALDEN; OR, LIFE IN THE WOODS, Henry David Thoreau. (0-486-28495-6)

NARRATIVE OF SOJOURNER TRUTH, Sojourner Truth. (0-486-29899-X)

THE WIT AND WISDOM OF MARK TWAIN: A Book of Quotations, Mark Twain. (0-486-40664-4)

UP FROM SLAVERY, Booker T. Washington. (0-486-28738-6)

A VINDICATION OF THE RIGHTS OF WOMAN, Mary Wollstonecraft. (0-486-29036-0)